His

Perfect Work

KATHY THOMAS

Published by: MIRACLE LANE Publishing, Oxford, Arkansas

Language: English

ISBN:0692889779
ISBN-13:9780692889770

And God's peace, which is far beyond human understanding, will keep your hearts and minds safe in union with Christ Jesus.

Philippians 4:7

HIS PERFECT WORK

DEDICATION

My husband David – my rock on this planet Earth. He waited on me hand and foot. He bathed me and dressed me. Cried with me. Prayed with me. Worried over me. He grumbled at times saying I'm not a nurse, all the while changing my dressings and cleaning my wounds. He drove me back and forth to every doctor's appointment. He drove me to work when I wasn't able to drive yet and waited on me to complete my work day. He walked with me through every step in this journey.

HIS PERFECT WORK

\

CHAPTERS

HIS PERFECT WORK

ACKNOWLEDGMENTS

Thank you to each and every person who encouraged me to write this book. I would like to say a special thank you to Luanne Gregory for the knowledge and wisdom she brought in the community college class on how to write a book. Thank you to Michele, Gaines, and Annie for being my editors. Since this is the first time I've given this a try, I'm sure that wasn't easy. Above all, thank you to my Lord and Savior Jesus Christ for dying on the cross for my sins. Without Him, answered prayers, and miracles, I would not be here to write this book. To God be all the glory.

Prologue

Miracles

Do you believe in miracles? An even better question, do you believe miracles still happen today? As you will glean from my story, my husband Dave and I believe.

According to Merriam-Webster, a miracle is a wonderful or unusual event caused by the power of God or an extraordinary event manifesting divine intervention in human affairs. I do believe the word miracle is overused in today's society. I don't believe it's a miracle when we get a great parking spot in front of the grocery store, or when that new the pair of boots we've been eyeing are miraculously on sale.

The miracles we read about in the Bible were extraordinary, divine, and unexplainable. Jesus walks on water, Balaam and his talking donkey, crossing of the Red Sea, Jesus feeds the five thousand, Jesus raises Lazarus from the dead, Joshua stops the sun, just to mention a few. These are huge, extraordinary, and unexplainable.

But now? Do we still have them now? Why wouldn't we? God is the same today as he was then. Why would He show His power then and not now? Why do we try to put God in a box? He is still all powerful. He still loves his children. "Jesus Christ is the same yesterday and today and forever." (Hebrews 13:8, NKJV)

I've heard stories that someone would have a diagnosis of terminal cancer and suddenly with the next radiology report it would be unexplainably gone. I've heard of and seen many real-life miracles. God has saved lives, healed physical illness, provided supernatural peace to the grieving heart, healed hearts full of pain and anger, changed hearts full of grudges, saved lost souls that were thought to be too bad to be saved, and saved marriages. If you start digging, you will find a lot of evidence of God's power in everyday human affairs.

Yes, still today. All things are possible with the power of God. His Word tells us so. "Jesus looked at them and said, with man this is impossible, but not with God, all things are possible with God". (Mark 10:27, NKJV) "I am the Lord, the God of all mankind, is anything too hard for me?" (Jeremiah 32:27, NKJV)

I believed in miracles, even before. It's different now; at times overwhelming. When I start to think about what happened to me, I well up with emotions, not because of the trauma or the pain but because of God's love for me. I've lay in bed at night and sobbed while telling God, *"Thank you, thank you God for the miracles."* I don't know why God chose me. I don't think it's for me to question. He did. He spared my life. He saved my arm. I am so thankful. I am so blessed.

Now it's up to me to share my story. There will be skeptics. There always has been and there always will be. I've told my story personally to a lot of people. I've had a variety of responses. Some tell me, "You are so lucky", while others tell me, "God isn't finished with you yet". Some look at me with disbelief.

Why did Dave place a street sign in our driveway called Miracle Lane? Because that's exactly what it is; a place where miracles happened. Every time I pull into the driveway, I smile. It brings me great joy to know that God loved this daughter so much that He provided her with such incredible blessings. There are many answered prayers in my story, but I also believe there were several extraordinary events, that were nothing short of miracles.

Chapter One

The Backstory

This is my story. A story I never planned to write. It's my recollection of events and emotions tied to an accident with a firearm, coupled with a few nuggets from my past, and some scriptures that spoke to my heart.

I've always dreamed of writing a book; however, this is not the story I imagined I would be telling. Before my accident, I was working on a manuscript for a fiction book. I was on the sixth chapter, and having so much fun writing. That book is still in my computer...unfinished.

On December 6, 2015, my life took a dramatic, unexpected turn. Because of this change in direction in my life, God laid it heavy on my heart to write it down. He spoke to my heart, saying, "*I want you to tell your story.*" My hope is that my story will touch your heart, and that you will allow God to use my story to draw you closer to Him. I hope it shows you that God can get you through the extremely tough times. This is a story of hope, miracles, healing, and perseverance.

The Roaring Lion

This is not a chapter I planned for my story. A few months after the accident, I was struggling to get dressed one day when God laid this subject on my heart. I felt God telling me, *"I want you to talk about the roaring lion. My people get complacent. Be on guard for the roaring lion."* My thoughts were, *No Lord, I don't want people to know about my past. They may judge me."* *"Don't worry about what other people think. You have been forgiven of your past, but are careful. The roaring lion will dredge it back up. He will use it against you. Keep Me in the forefront as you write about it."* In my heart, I continued to argue with God. It took a long time for me to decide to add this chapter. It was difficult. It continued to lay heavy on my heart, so I thought I better follow His lead.

Peter warns us in this scripture to be alert; our enemy is always looking for ways to devour us. "Be sober, be vigilant; because your adversary, the devil, walks about like a roaring lion, seeking whom he may devour."(1 Peter 5:8, NKJV) He looks hardest at those drawing closer to our Savior. He is not worried about us before we're saved. He's got us then. He wants us most after we've given our heart to Jesus. He thinks, *If I can only draw them back to me.*

He hates it when we start working for Jesus; when we become a servant for Jesus; when we study our Bible; when we teach a Sunday school class; when we work in the sound booth at church; when we mow the church lawn; when we host a small group Bible study in our home; when we go to the mission field. He doesn't want us to do any of that. He wants us to be lukewarm. He is hiding and waiting for some big event to happen in our life like an accident, a death in the family, a divorce, or a miscarriage. These are all opportunities for the enemy to devour us. That's why Peter warns us to be on guard. In the most crucial times in our life; when we are going through tragedy and sorrow, we have to be on guard.

Regina

The devil will also take an opportunity to devour us if we don't heed God's leading. Sometimes, God tries to lead us in a certain direction. Sometimes, we do not listen. We want our own selfish way. This very thing happened to my sister, Regina.

Regina was ten years older than me, and I thought she hung the moon. She was on fire for Jesus at a young age. She had an incredible singing voice. In her early twenties, she traveled all over Arkansas singing and preaching about God. She also desperately wanted to find a husband and have a child.

She met a man and, after a short period of time together, they planned to get married. She knew in her heart this marriage was not in the will of God. She felt God pleading with her, *Don't do this.* The day of her wedding, God tried to warn her of this mistake through numerous mishaps, including a tire blowout on the way to the wedding venue. She got out of her car and screamed at God, "You are not stopping me! Get out of my life! I'm marrying this man!" God did just that. Satan took over. She was devoured.

Her life was never the same. She did marry him and was pregnant right away. She left him before the baby was born. She drifted completely away from God. She was in one toxic relationship after another. She and a male friend were parked in a car with it running. Both suffered carbon monoxide poisoning and died. She was gone, at age twenty-nine...leaving behind a four-year-old daughter. Be on guard!

The Wild Child

How is this relevant to my story? You see, Satan also had me for many years. I don't remember going to church as a young child but maybe a few times with my friend, Kathy. My parents never took me to church. I remember going to church with Regina as a preteen and teenager. As an evangelist in a charismatic type of church, she took me all over the place with her.

I remember getting saved and baptized as a young preteen, but I always felt inadequate because I couldn't speak in tongues. The church that Regina attended taught us speaking in tongues was a requirement to be filled with the Holy Ghost. It seems I got saved and baptized every year for several years at church camp, but never made it to the Holy Ghost filling part. Judging by my behavior in my teen years, I clearly didn't have a change of heart.

I was a wild child. I know some of the folks reading this book are shaking their heads right now thinking, *No way. She's too much of a rule follower*. That hasn't always been the case. Between ages fourteen and sixteen, I smoked a lot of marijuana, drank of lot of Easy Days, Mellow Nights, and Boone's Farm Strawberry Hill wine. My best friend, Kathy, and I were two crazy, wild chicks.

At age sixteen, that all came to a screeching halt when I became pregnant with my first son, Jeremy. I had to grow up very fast. Proms and graduation were replaced with diapers and sleepless nights. I dropped out of high school in the eleventh grade, and married my son's father. I took the GED test and received a high school diploma. I did life the hard way.

My first husband and his family were members of the Church of Christ. My husband, our son, Jeremy, and I were living in the Church of Christ parsonage in Tyronza, Arkansas when my second child, Amy, was born. It was in this home that I received the call from my mom telling me Regina had died. I still remember the pain in her voice. Regina's age made her a mother figure to me, so her death was extremely difficult to bear. Her four-year-old daughter, April, moved in with us shortly after. I was nineteen with two children of my own, and raising my late sister's child.

The church was having a gospel meeting. The preacher spoke to me after the service telling me I needed to give my life to Jesus. He was pushy, and annoying. I was pregnant with my daughter Amy. I was miserable and hormonal. I got baptized again that night, honestly just to shut him up, hoping he would leave me alone. Just another time that I went through the motions of being saved...but all I really did was get wet.

I had my youngest son, Josh, at age twenty-two. By that time, we had moved to Jonesboro where, at age twenty-six, I enrolled in the Arkansas State University (ASU) nursing program. For most of my kids' lives, they were raised attending Church of Christ. After a number of years, I divorced the father of my children.

My niece, April, who we had adopted, sought after her natural father and moved in with him. That was very painful for me. I felt like I let my sister down. I was a young, divorced mom raising my three children.

Through all of this, I obtained my nursing degree from ASU at age twenty-nine. I had just been a nurse for a year when my dad became sick with sepsis secondary to rheumatoid arthritis and died at age sixty-six. Just a few years after dad died, my mom moved in with me. She had never worked, or even driven a car. She was lost without dad.

Moving On

When my kids were all teenagers, I married again and began attending a Baptist Church. I was baptized again and really thought this time was real. Now that I think back, I know God was not priority one. Yes, we went to church, but He was not first. Not first in my marriage; not first in my life. I don't think He was even second, third, or fourth. I was focused on myself, my career, and going back to school to get a bachelor's and master's degree. I was also focused on kids, basketball games, and taking care of my mom.

Please don't misunderstand, all those are important. They are important to God, too. The point is, He comes first. All the other falls into place. He should be the center. It's a relationship with us He seeks. I was putting Him on a shelf and bringing Him out on Sundays. I let my guard down. That marriage failed, too. The roaring lion definitely jumped in.

Most of my adulthood, I was self-deceived. I claimed to be a Christian, but my life sure did not show it. I lost track of how many times I was baptized. I'm proof that getting dunked under the water does nothing but get you wet if there isn't a true and honest change of heart. There was no fruit. There was no relationship. I know now that my claim to be a Christian was a lie. "If we say that we have fellowship with Him, and walk in darkness, we lie, and do not practice the truth." (1 John 1:6, NKJV)

David

Then I met Dave. We both had prior marriages. We both caused a lot of pain in our children's lives. One of my biggest regrets is all the pain I caused my children. I am so thankful for grace. I am so thankful for the grace from my Father in Heaven and from my children.

Dave and I married, but we were definitely not living for Jesus. We were very far from it. Satan also had Dave for many years. Like me, he never really went to church as a child. In fact, other than attending a few times with his mom as a small child, he had never really been in church at all. Dave was a heavy drinker, nearly every day. Honestly, I didn't think this marriage would make it either. I wasn't going to spend the rest of my life living with a drunk. Dave said many times, "I have no intention of stopping, I like to drink." Satan had a very strong hold on us.

From Darkness to Light

In December 2011, on a Saturday night, out of the blue, Dave said, "We're going to church tomorrow." You could have literally knocked me over with a feather. Where did that come from? To this day, I think someone was praying for Dave; probably his mother. We drove around in our little Arkansas town of Oxford and looked for churches. Then we went to Salem, about 20 minutes away, and drove around looking for churches. We were about to give up when we saw the church on the hill as we were leaving

Salem. Dave said, "Wait! That's it, right there!" We pulled in the parking lot of Salem First Baptist Church and Dave got out seeing if he could find service times. He got back in the car and said, "This is it." Satan must've been working on me, because I objected, "No. This church is too big." We did go to church that next day. When we walked out, we looked at each other and agreed this was home. From that day forward, we knew this was where we belonged.

On February 26, 2012, Dave and I gave our lives to Jesus. We were both baptized. This was real! It was a true conversion. I could feel the Holy Spirit in my soul. Our lives have not been the same since. It was like someone flipped a switch from darkness to light. All the pain that we caused, and the track records we had accumulated were all wiped clean.

From February 2012 to December 2015, we continued to grow in our relationship with Jesus. We loved going to church, but going to church was not something we packed up and sat on a shelf from Sunday to Sunday. It's was a true relationship with God. Going to church allowed us to worship and praise Him. It allowed us to fellowship with our brothers and sisters. It allowed us to dig into His Word. A relationship with God was in every fiber of our being. It was in every decision we made.

Our New Home

Now that you know my backstory, I will get to the part where the devil was looming like the roaring lion, hoping to derail my relationship with God. We were living in a small mobile home on ten acres. It was difficult for our kids and grandkids to come and spend much time because of the lack of space. The house next door, which was larger than our house, came up for sale. It sat on two acres that looked like it had been cut out of the corner of our ten acres. We started praying. We prayed for guidance and wisdom, asking if we should purchase the house next door. We prayed that if it was meant to be, it would all fall into place. If not, we would accept that, too. He answered. It all fell into place. We bought the house next door. We made a promise to God that we would have small group Bible study in our new home. We wanted to use our home to glorify Him.

We bought our home in November 2015, and had not yet fully moved in when a tragic accident nearly took my life. We could've gone the opposite direction after the accident. We could have let Satan get a strong hold on us again. We could have questioned God saying, "Why did this happen?" Not even for a split second did we question God. If it was Satan's plan to derail us and get us off track because we were growing so strong in Jesus, he failed! This accident had the opposite effect. It caused our faith to grow even stronger.

Chapter Two

The Unforgettable Day

December 6, 2015

It was a Sunday, a beautiful, warm, sunny day in December. Dave and I went to church that morning. We were very excited because, after church, we planned to move into the new home we had just closed on two weeks before. We moved several loads of furniture and were all set to spend the night in our new home. The plan was to move one more load, clean up, and go to the outdoor drama at church that evening.

Dave had several guns he wanted to move on the last load over. He said he would just put them in the metal cabinet and move the cabinet. I said, "Why don't you just let me carry some of them." One of the guns was a .357 magnum that Dave had taken with him deer hunting, and it was still loaded. He was insistent on putting them in the cabinet to move. I was being stubborn and wanted to carry them. I looped the .357 magnum over my shoulder and Dave insisted I bring the holster over my head, he said, "it's more stable that way." I was set. I hopped on the red trailer that Dave was pulling with our four-wheeler, with our last load. My arms were around the gun cabinet so it wouldn't fall over.

We were laughing and having so much fun that afternoon. In a split second everything changed. We were suddenly thrust into an unknown world. It was a world we would've never dreamed of; a world where the presence of God showed up immediately.

The Gunshot

We were three fourths of way to the new home with the last load when I heard the gunshot. It was deafening. I couldn't imagine where that shot came from. I did not know immediately that I was shot. Then I looked down and saw my left arm and felt the pain. The .357 Magnum, with a hunting round in it, had fallen out of the holster and landed on the trailer causing it to discharge.

Dave was beside me by now. He was screaming, "Oh my God baby, what happened!" I really didn't know. All I knew was that I was shot, in incredible pain, and bleeding.

There was a huge hole through the center of my arm at the bend of the elbow. I'm told the hunting round was significant to the injury because it expanded on impact causing a much larger exit wound. I couldn't move my left hand, it was dangling. We could see daylight through my arm. In that moment, I thought I would lose my arm, or maybe even my life, because of blood loss.

The Trailer

I tried to hold pressure, but my right hand was too small to reach around my arm. I told Dave, "You have to find a tourniquet." Being a nurse, I knew if there was an artery involved, I could bleed out in a matter of minutes. Dave pleaded, "No! I've got to call 911!" Which was true, but I felt a tourniquet was needed first. We argued over it for a couple of seconds.

I asked Dave to lay me down on the trailer we were using to move and put my feet up, he did, and went to find a tourniquet, while calling 911 at the same time. Dave came back with a man's belt and placed it on my upper arm for a tourniquet.

Dave kept checking on me because I was so quiet. He kept asking me, "Are you okay?" He also kept looking me over for more injuries, asking, "Are you hurting anywhere else?" He said over and over, "I am so sorry." I could see the pain and worry in his eyes. It hurt my heart to see David in so much pain and agony over me. He had a lost look on his face. I wanted to help him, to make him feel better, but I couldn't.

While lying on the trailer, still waiting for the ambulance, I asked Dave to bring me my cell phone. I knew the hospital, which was also my employer, needed to be aware that I was on my way. I knew a surgeon needed be ready and waiting. After fumbling with my phone for what seemed like forever, because I could only use one hand, I was able to get in touch with Holly, the house supervisor. I told Holly that I accidentally shot myself and that we would be coming in by ambulance, and that I would need a surgeon.

Dave told me later there was a lot of blood on the trailer. He told me that one of our neighbors made the statement; they had never seen that much blood. I can imagine it was a pretty frightful scene. I was unaware. My physical awareness while lying on the trailer was pain, being cold, and having a very dry mouth. A first responder from Oxford Fire Department brought one of those shiny silver blankets and put it over me. That felt very good. I am thankful for first responders.

It seemed like it took a long time for the ambulance to arrive. I was thinking they must've been on another run. Much later after the accident Dave and I viewed the security camera videos and discovered it took twenty-two minutes for the ambulance to arrive to our home.

At least three people on the scene questioned me, asking what happened. I'm not sure who they were. I would guess the police, the first responder, and the folks on the ambulance. Someone asked me if I felt threatened. I'm guessing that was the police, wanting to make sure this was an accident.

Pain

As I was lying on the trailer, in extreme pain like I had never felt before, I was thinking about Jesus. The pain I was in was unimaginable. It felt unbearable. But there was nothing I could do but bear it. I kept thinking over and over about the pain Jesus must've gone through on the cross for me. What I was going through didn't even come close to what He went through. My suffering was not worthy to be compared to what he went through on the cross, but I couldn't help but go there. My heart ached knowing the pain that I was feeling was only a minuscule portion of how Jesus suffered for this undeserving daughter.

It didn't really take very long for them to get me loaded up on the ambulance once they arrived. I was on my way. I knew if I could get to my hospital, White River Medical Center (WRMC), they would take very good care of me. David was allowed to ride in the ambulance with me. I was very thankful. I did not want to leave him behind.

The paramedic with me was very kind and compassionate. She wanted to give me pain medication; however after checking my vital signs she told me she couldn't due to my low blood pressure. I told her I understood. As she continued to check my blood pressure, she told me she was going to have to put the tourniquet back on because my blood pressure was dropping. She told me it was going to be more painful. Just when I thought the pain couldn't get any worse, it did. The tourniquet literally felt like it was taking my arm off.

Emergency Room

I arrived in the emergency department at WRMC to see a room full of familiar faces. I'm not exactly sure who all was there, but I do remember seeing my son Josh, daughter-in-law Kristine and grandson, Isaac, our pastor Brother John and his wife Sister Sandy, two hospital administrators; one of which was my administrator, Gary Paxson and Robert Wright. I was so blessed to have this crowd by my side.

I remember looking across the trauma room, seeing my David, leaned over with his head in his hands, and Brother John's hand on Dave's back. I was so thankful in that moment that God provided us with a great pastor who shows up and tends to those in pain.

Two surgeons were waiting for me when I arrived. I heard Dr. Allen telling Dr. Abraham, "She's one of ours." I smiled when I heard that. It's amazing how words can make you feel. I remember Mr. Paxson standing beside the stretcher, telling me he would be praying for me. All the words of encouragement were like logs added to a fire. They surrounded me with an incredible warm feeling.

It didn't seem like I was in the emergency room very long when Dr. Allen came and told me the injuries were too big to be fixed at my local hospital. He said I would need to be flown to the University of Arkansas for Medical Science, Medical Center

(UAMS, Medical Center) in Little Rock. He assured me that he knew just the surgeon at UAMS who could take care of this. I was told the surgeon was one of the top ten elbow and shoulder surgeons in the country, and he happened to be on call. I don't believe in happenstance.

Helicopter Ride

Survival Flight has only been at WRMC for a relatively, short period of time. When it first arrived, I made the statement, "You will never catch me on a helicopter." Boy, did I have to eat those words. And, not only did you catch me on a helicopter, I was very thankful for it.

The flight nurses were Stanley and Johnny; they were very confident, yet compassionate. They checked on me often and were able to give me pain medication. The pilot of the helicopter was Katrina. She told me that she had flown in the military for many years. I felt very safe and in good hands.

Dave rode with me on the ambulance, leaving him with no transportation to Little Rock. He didn't have his wallet, or even a coat. He initially asked someone in the emergency room if he could fly in the helicopter with me and was told no. Just before they were getting ready to load me on the helicopter one of the flight nurses asked Dave if he had ever flown in a helicopter. His answer was, "I've jumped out of helicopters; I was in Air Assault in the Army." "Good, you're going with us, was the flight nurses reply."

I was already in the helicopter when Dave boarded and told me he was going to get to fly with me. Immediately my personality kicked in, the type of personality that wants to organize and be sure we're following the rules. As soon as Dave sat in his seat, I started adding in my head how much weight the helicopter was carrying. I was thinking, *okay I know Dave weighs this much and I weigh this much and the pilot probably weighs this much, and so on and so forth.* It's kind of funny now when I think about it and I tell the story, but it really wasn't at the time. Actually, I was thrilled that Dave was going to be at my side.

UAMS, Medical Center

When I arrived at UAMS, Medical Center, I was taken immediately for CT scans. Afterward, I was greeted in the ER by a resident. He was very kind and thoughtful. He informed me that I had a very extensive wound and that I would need to go to surgery immediately. He told me Dr. Ahmadi was an excellent surgeon and that he would be taking very good care of me. He also told me that I was very "lucky" because I have a huge hole in the center of my arm at the elbow and the main arteries were untouched. I remember telling him, "I'm not lucky, I am blessed."

Dr. Ahmadi, the surgeon, also saw me in the emergency room. By this time, it was very late in the evening. He was very professional, kind, and compassionate. He explained everything that was about to happen. He told me I would need several surgeries. The first surgery was to clean the wound of debris and take a look at what he has to work with. Dave shared with me later that Dr. Ahmadi said this was a first for him. He had never seen an elbow wound that he could see daylight through. I went to surgery and woke up on the fifth floor at UAMS, Medical Center. Dave was by my side. It was the end of that unforgettable day...a day full of miracles.

HIS PERFECT WORK

Chapter Three

Three Miracles

Miracle One, The Cap

It could have been a very different Christmas for my husband, my children, and my grandchildren that year, but God spared my life that day. For that I am very thankful. I am blessed.

I was wearing a cap to keep my hair out of my face while we were moving. I had the cap on backwards; the bill in the back, probably to aggravate my husband because he doesn't like to see people wear caps backwards.

Sometime after the accident Dave shared with me just how close of a call this really was. He told me there was blood and tissue all over my face and my glasses. The cap I was wearing that day was blown off my head. Let that sink in...I had the cap on backwards.

I wondered why Dave kept asking me, while I was lying on the trailer, if I was hurting anywhere else. How did that bullet pass my face and blow off my cap without causing a scratch on my face or head and how was I unaware?

I was sitting in church sometime after the accident when one of the older men from our church, who is a deacon, turned around in his pew and told me what a miracle I am. He said to me, "You know God was in control of the direction of that bullet." I smiled and said yes, "He absolutely was." I'm not saying by any means that God caused this accident. But I do believe, with all of my heart, that He took control the very split second the bullet left that gun.

Picture This

A bullet discharges from a gun...goes though the elbow that's resting next to the abdomen...leaving a huge hole in the elbow. The bullet misses the arteries...misses the abdomen...travels toward the face...leaving a trail of blood and tissue on the face and head. The bullet misses the face, but blows off the cap, that's on the head, backwards. Happenstance? No way! I would like to see that scene recreated on that TV show that busts the myths.

Miracle Two, The Belt

Remember me saying I sent Dave to find a tourniquet? From the hole in my arm and the amount of blood I saw, I was sure the main artery was hit. I knew I was in grave danger, and that I could die in a matter of minutes. Dave ran into our new home and remembered the only thing we had moved was large pieces of furniture; no small items. He made a quick run through the house and could find nothing to use for a tourniquet. He normally wears a belt, but that day he hadn't.

We were working in the house for the past couple of weeks painting and putting up crown molding. All of the supplies we needed for painting were kept in the laundry room. We were in and out of that laundry room numerous times in the last two weeks. Dave was about to give up on finding a tourniquet when he decided to run through the house one more time. As he ran past the laundry room he saw something shiny out of the corner of his eye. It was a belt hanging on the backside of a shelf in the laundry room. It was about 12 to 15 feet away from where he was standing; it was amazing that he could even see the belt.

Numerous times in the past two weeks we were in and out that laundry room and we never saw the belt. Had we seen it, we would have moved it to the pile next to the back door, where we were placing items left by the previous owners.

I was holding my arm with the other hand to try to slow the bleeding to this point. I have very small hands and I knew that would be inadequate to slow the bleeding. Dave placed the belt on my upper arm for a tourniquet. It took a long time for the ambulance to arrive, by that time the bleeding had slowed. I know God hid that belt from us until we needed it. Then it shined!

Miracle Three, The Artery

Take a look at any anatomy textbook, you will find the brachial artery is large, and it runs through the center of the arm. You can feel it pulsing, if you try. Take your index and middle finger and put it in the bend of your arm at the elbow; you should be able to feel a pulse, the beat of your heart. This is where a nurse places the stethoscope when they take your blood pressure. This was the path of the bullet. The bones in my upper arm and lower arm, near the elbow, were shattered. How did the bullet miss the arteries?

The doctors really never told me exactly how much blood I lost, if they did, I don't remember. They just said you've lost a lot of blood. I know I was extremely weak. Sometime later I was able to look at my lab work on my patient electronic health record. It was very eye-opening; I lost nearly half of my blood that day. Without the belt and God's protection of the brachial artery and my very life, it would've been a very different ending to the story. I wouldn't be here to share His glory, power, healing, and miracles.

His Power

I won't believe the cap, the belt, and the artery were just a coincidence. I know different. I know His power. I know His love. I know His promise. I know there is absolutely nothing too big for God. I don't know the exact reason that He spared my life and spared my arm that day. But I know He knows the reason. If my story touches one heart or makes the difference in one life, everything I went through was worth it. I want others to experience the peace that I felt that day when they are caught in the middle of a tragedy. I want others to trust Him when they are falling apart. So, can God change the trajectory of a bullet? Can God seal an artery? Can God provide a tourniquet when and where we need it? Can God provide supernatural peace in the midst of tragedy? You bet He can. And He did.

Chapter Four

Supernatural Peace

There are many scriptures in the Bible about peace. It's a special kind of peace. Not the kind of peace you're speaking of when you say something like, "it's so peaceful on my back porch", "or it's such a peaceful night." No. This peace I speak of is different...very different. I can't comprehend it. I'm not sure that I can find the words to articulate it, but I will do my best.

I never experienced it before the accident, especially in the way that I'm about to describe. It's the kind of peace spoken of in His Word. "The LORD will give strength to his people; the Lord will bless his people with peace." (Psalm 29:11, NKJV) "Peace I leave with you, My peace I give to you; not as the world gives do I give to you. Let not your heart be troubled." (John 14:27, NKJV) The kind of peace I would imagine Daniel experienced as he was in the lion's den. Or Shadrach, Meshach, and Abednego were experiencing in the fiery furnace. Or Paul and Silas as they were singing as prisoners in that Roman jail. It's the kind of peace you feel when you're in the middle of something unimaginable, yet you know with all of your heart that God's got this.

Miracle Four

God provided me with supernatural peace the instant that bullet hit my arm. I never screamed. I never cried. I remained calm and alert. Dave was not calm. I could hear Dave talking to God very boldly saying, "Don't you take her from me". Not me. I was calm. My heart was not racing. It was as if I could hear a voice in my heart, telling me, "*You are okay*." "*No matter what happens, you are okay.*" "*I've got this.*" I believed that voice, and I was absolutely, okay.

The Worrier

Let me tell you why this is extraordinary and a miracle. I am a worrier. I worry about everything. I come from a long line of worriers. My grandma, my mom, and my sister were all worriers. If we didn't have something to worry about, that in itself was a worry. It was not at all normal for me to be calm and worry free.

I am not an emergency room nurse because I can't think fast on my feet. I don't like the adrenaline rush. It worries me. I need time to process things, to think about things. That day I was totally calm and at peace. I calmly asked Dave to find something for a tourniquet, call 911, and lay me down and prop up my feet. I asked Dave to hand me my cell phone, and I called the hospital where I work and told them to get the surgical team ready because I had accidentally shot myself in my arm. When the ambulance arrived, I told the paramedic that I needed a large bore IV to the right arm, with 1000 milliliters of normal saline, running as fast as they could get it, because I was dry. Where did that come from? It was like a scene from one of those emergency TV dramas. Again, that wasn't normal for me.

As I lay on the trailer, in extreme pain, waiting on the ambulance, with my feet propped up, and the tourniquet on my arm. I felt a peace come over me. It was a peace like I had never felt before; though I was physically cold, I felt as if I was wrapped in a warm blanket of God's love. I heard in my heart again, *"Everything is going to be okay."* *"No matter what happens, you are okay."* I was calm. I wasn't crying. I wasn't screaming in pain. I didn't feel anxious. I didn't feel nervous. I didn't feel worried. I felt covered by His love and grace.

I worry about flying, which is why I stated earlier that I would never willingly fly in the new helicopter. I really didn't know what to expect as I was being airlifted to UAMS, Medical Center in Little Rock, but I knew whatever was ahead of me, God was with me. I was at total peace with the flight.

There is no explanation for the peace that I was feeling. It was the peace that passes all understanding, the peace that Paul talked about in his letter to the Philippians. "And God's peace, which is far beyond human understanding, will keep your hearts and minds safe in union with Christ Jesus." (Philippians 4:7, GNB) It absolutely did just that.

In the days to come after the accident, the nurse became a patient. I faced many scary things, each time with God by my side giving me a peace that surpassed all understanding. In this journey, I had five surgeries, which normally, I would worry and worry over. Not this time. God had this. From the very second that gun discharged...God had this!

Chapter Five

Nurse Becomes Patient

I am very thankful for all the kindness, compassion, and care provided to me from all the healthcare providers involved in my journey. From the first responders, paramedics, emergency room staff at White River Medical Center, Survival Flight crew, nurses, doctors, physical therapists, radiology staff, UAMS, Medical Center staff, the list goes on and on...I had great caregivers.

Five Days at UAMS, Medical Center

I was treated at UAMS, Medical Center for five days. It was a difficult week, but I never lost my peace or joy. I had three surgeries that week, one on Sunday to irrigate and clean debris from the wound, one on Tuesday for irrigation and debridement, and one on Thursday to place the external fixation device. The injuries to my arm included: closed fracture of the ulna, complete tear of lateral collateral ligament of the elbow, fracture of the humerus, fracture of the radial neck, major osseous defect of the left humerus, and radial nerve trauma. Basically, to put it in layman's terms, my elbow was gone, all the bones around it were broken, the ligament was torn apart, and the radial nerve was missing about two inches.

I was very weak, having lost about half of my blood. I felt like I weighed a thousand pounds. It took every ounce of energy to get out of that bed and walk to the bathroom. I forced myself to get up and walk in the halls. The nurse in me knew it was not an option to stay in that bed because of potential complications from immobility.

My doctors came to see us every day. I tried to recruit the resident doctor to come work at my hospital. After the second surgery to clean the wound, the surgeon told Dave and me there were three options to fix my arm.

1. Fuse it all together and let it heal. I would be unable to use my arm after it healed. To me this wasn't even an option.

2. An artificial elbow that would heal relatively quickly, but I could only lift five pounds with that arm for the rest of my life. I didn't like that idea. We have lots of grandkids, and at the time, a new grandbaby on the way. Being a grandma requires a functioning elbow that can lift more than five pounds.

3. An allograft, which was replacing my elbow with a donor,

cadaver bone. Once healed, there would be no weight limitations. This was my surgeon's recommendation.

I chose the third option, the allograft surgery. This surgery couldn't be done immediately. I would have to wear something called an external fixator to hold my bones together for healing for about eight weeks. The allograft surgery would have to be done in January. The surgeon also told us the radial nerve would need repaired. That would take another surgery called a nerve transfer and another surgeon.

For the first three days of the week, I had the same nurse, Sarah. I liked her and was glad to see her back each day that she worked. She was a good listener with a great attitude. She always remembered how I preferred to take my medicine, which is a big deal for someone that struggles with that.

I had a total of five surgeries. I had three the week of the accident, the fourth on December 23rd to repair the nerve, and the fifth, the allograft surgery, on January 25th. The care was always excellent at UAMS, Medical Center.

Memories of that Long Week

Some things stand out about that week in the hospital. With each surgery, came post-operative pain. The first two surgeries to clean the wound of debris didn't seem too bad. I was given some type of nerve block while in recovery, that I became very fond of.

It worked very well after those first two surgeries and the pain was minimal. The third surgery to place the external fixator was longer and the pain was very tough afterwards. I did receive the nerve block, but it didn't work as well as before. I didn't get much relief and I was miserable for a while.

Josh and Jeremy, my two sons, brought me sushi served with a side of humor that only they can bring. My boys can make me laugh like no one else. Laughter is good medicine, especially when you're in pain. I was very thankful for my sons, the sushi, and the humor.

My heart ached for my daughter Amy. She was unable to come to the hospital because she was several hours away in Missouri, and in nursing school, having all of her finals that week. Knowing my baby girl the way I do, it was very difficult for her to not be able to come to the hospital to be with her mamma. I prayed for Amy, for God to give her peace and help her with her finals.

Dave and Jeremy left on Monday to get Dave's truck. I felt lost in that hospital room without Dave. It seemed like a long day. I spent time praying for their safe return to the hospital and thanking God for my life and my arm.

Dave and I had a visit from the hospital chaplain that week. She spent quite a bit of time with us talking about Jesus and praying. There's something very sustaining about spending some time talking about Jesus with a sister in Christ.

Patient Again

I went back to UAMS, Medical Center for two more surgeries; the nerve transfer surgery and the allograft surgery. The nerve transfer was a one-day surgery, not requiring a stay in the hospital. The allograft was a long surgery and was supposed to be a one-night stay, but it turned into a two-night stay. I was very sick after that surgery. I felt terrible. I felt like I was full of fluid. I was vomiting and just overall felt lousy and in pain. I was still not feeling well when I was discharged, and I dreaded the long ride home. I was thankful that I slept most of the way.

Lots of Love

We were shown a lot of love from family, brothers and sisters in Christ, friends, and co-workers through lots of prayers, cards, flowers, text messages, and phone calls. I am very thankful for the outpouring of love. It warmed our hearts and touched our souls.

Many times, I heard the words, "you are so lucky." I always gave my standard answer, "I'm not lucky, I am blessed." Even though it was tough times, I remember being full of joy, that God spared my life and showed me his power.

Chapter Six

There is Power In His Name

She touched the hem of his garment. That's all it took; one touch. Her faith in Him is all she needed. He made her well. I love this story told by Matthew.

"And suddenly, a woman who had a flow of blood for twelve years came from behind and touched the hem of His garment. For she said to herself, "*if only I may touch His garment, I shall be made well.*" But Jesus turned around, and when He saw her he said, "Be of good cheer, daughter; your faith has made you well." And the woman was made well from that hour." (Matthew 9:20-22, NKJV) Immediately she was healed. "Daughter, your faith has made you well." That's all it took, one touch of faith.

Even though we can't physically reach out and touch Jesus, we can call His name. There is power in His name. That's exactly what I did. Two weeks after the allograft surgery to replace my elbow, Dave had taken me back to Little Rock to see my surgeon. During that appointment, they removed the stitches from the inner and outer parts of my arm. There were many, many stitches. It was quite painful, and I was feeling a little queasy during the process. We left and headed back home.

Feeling Ill

Dave wanted to stop at Sam's Club to pick up a few items. I should've gone with my first instinct to stay in the car. I was only two weeks out from another major surgery. But, I didn't go with my instinct, and I decided to go into Sam's with Dave.

We had not been in the store very long when I begin to feel ill. I felt cold and clammy and thought any minute I was going to be in the floor. I told Dave, "I'm going to go up front and sit where they sell pizza and drinks." I didn't even tell him how I was feeling. This was really a stupid thing for me to do. I made my way to the front of the store; we were at the back of the store when I started feeling bad.

I sat down at one of the picnic tables in the pizza area. I could feel myself about to lose consciousness. So many things were going through my mind. I was thinking, "*I'm about to pass out, people will surround me, they are going to call an ambulance, and I am headed back to Little Rock*". I thought, "*No way, this is not good*". "*I do not want to take an ambulance ride back to the hospital. I do not want people surrounding me.*" All the while I felt myself drifting further and further into a state of losing consciousness. I was nauseous, cold, clammy, and lightheaded.

Call His Name

I began to say the name, "*Jesus.*" First I would say it in my head. Then I begin to say it out loud over and over and over and over again. *"Jesus, Jesus, Jesus, Jesus, Jesus."* I literally sat there for the remaining time while Dave shopped, probably 20 minutes, saying the name Jesus. I began to feel better. My head stopped spinning. I became warm. My nausea went away. I saw David at the check-out counter, walked over to him, and we walked to the car. I laid my head back, told him I hadn't been feeling well, and slept the rest of the way home.

There is absolute power in the name of Jesus. I have no doubt I would have been laid up in an ambulance headed back to the hospital in Little Rock had I not called His name. The woman who touched the hem of his garment taught us about that power. She taught us that faith in Jesus can get us through the toughest of situations.

Something About that Name

Jesus! There's just something about that name! "And there is salvation in no one else, for there is no other name under Heaven given among men by which we must be saved." (Acts 4:12, ESV) How incredible is that! No other name under Heaven!

The name Jesus, writers still write about it and singers still sing about it today. As I sat and thought about the name of Jesus, beautiful songs came to mind. "Jesus, Jesus, Jesus, There's Just Something about That Name", by Bill and Gloria Gaither. The 7eventh Time Down song, "When you don't know what to say Just Say Jesus, There is power in the name, The Name of Jesus."

As I was lay in bed thinking about the name of Jesus, I drifted off to sleep. I woke up in the middle of the night with another song in my head. It was the song by Hill Song United, "What a Wonderful Name It Is." I challenge you to sit quietly and listen to these songs and let the words sink into your soul. They remind us how beautiful, wonderful, and powerful is the name of Jesus.

His Power

I felt led to write this chapter about the power in the name of Jesus. I hope my experience and the words on these pages will help you in your darkest hour. It may be a physical experience like I had. It may be an emotional moment. I've had plenty of those. It may be a time when you're trying to make a decision in your life. It may be when you're in the middle of a crisis or emergency. The possibilities are endless.

I'm reminded of a sermon from our pastor, Brother John. He spoke about suffering, stating it is inevitable. In this life we are going to have tragedies, suffering, physical and emotional pain. Through this we can reach out to Jesus. Jesus gives us hope. Jesus is our hope. As a Christian, we can claim that hope. We have instant access. Let these scriptures remind you of His power.

"Our suffering is light and temporary and is producing for us an eternal glory that is greater than anything we can imagine." (2 Corinthians 4:17, GWB)

"When she heard about Jesus, she came behind Him in the crowd and touched His garment. For she said, "If only I may touch His clothes, I shall be made well." (Mark 5:28, NKJV)

"Wherever He entered, into villages, cities, or the country, they laid the sick in the marketplaces, and begged Him that they might just touch the hem of His garment. And as many as touched Him were made well." (Mark 6:56, NKJV)

"Then He came to Bethsaida; and they brought a blind man to Him, and begged Him to touch him." (Mark 8:22, NKJV)

"And begged Him that they might only touch the hem of His garment. And as many as touched it were made perfectly well." (Matthew 14:36, NKJV)

Through my recovery and healing, prayer and scriptures were my comfort, my peace, and my food to get me through every day.

HIS PERFECT WORK

Chapter Seven

Recovery and Healing

Recovery and healing are still a work in progress. It's been almost two years since my accident and while I have full use of my arm, shoulder and elbow, the radial nerve transfer is still healing. It has made slow progress. I still can't use the computer keyboard or clap my hands. I have use of my left hand; I just can't lift it or straighten my fingers. The radial nerve may never totally heal. I'm okay with that.

The Thorn in the Flesh

It makes me think of Paul. He had something that God wouldn't take away. He called it a thorn in his flesh. "So to keep me from becoming conceited because of the surpassing greatness of the revelations, a thorn was given me in the flesh, a messenger of Satan to harass me, to keep me from becoming conceited. Three times I pleaded with the Lord about this, that it should leave me.

But he said to me, My grace is sufficient for you, for my power is made perfect in weakness. Therefore I will boast all the more gladly of my weaknesses, so that the power of Christ may rest upon me. For the sake of Christ, then, I am content with weaknesses, insults, hardships, persecutions, and calamities. For when I am weak, then I am strong." (2 Corinthians 12: 7-10, ESV)

I never want to forget the miracles and healing that God provided. I want to remain humble. I'm okay with a reminder that God is still working in my life. I am blessed.

Healing Takes Time

For those of you reading this book who might be going through the healing process for some type of injury or accident or even an emotional wound trying to heal, there's one thing that I hope you take away from my experience. Here it is. It's profound. **Don't rush it, healing takes time.** God created these bodies and hearts. He knows it takes time. We as humans tend to want to rush things. I felt a nagging at my heart many times during this healing process that said, *slow down*. I caught myself over and over trying to do things before my body was ready. Which in the long run we all know, does more harm than good.

God's Timing

Trust God's timing. There are many examples in His Word where our timing and God's timing may differ. But if we trust God's timing, He will always come through. I am reminded about the story of Abraham, Sarah and Isaac.

God made a promise to Abraham that he and Sarah would have a child. Sarah even laughed about the promise, signifying doubt in Sarah's heart. Abraham had doubts too. How could Sarah and Abraham bear a child in their old age? God told Abraham they would have a child, yet nothing happened.

Abraham and Sarah even plotted and took the matter in their own hands with Sarah's handmade, Hagar, bearing a child, Ishmael. Abraham and Sarah had to wait a very long time, but in God's perfect timing, God came through and Isaac was born. But just like Abraham and Sarah, we try to rush things. We ignore God's timing and often try to fix things on our own.

"And he said, I will certainly return unto thee according to the time of life; and, behold, Sarah, thy wife, shall have a son. Sarah was listening in the tent door which was behind him. Is anything too hard for the LORD? At the time appointed I will return unto thee, according to the time of life." (Genesis 18:10, 14, NKJV)

"And the LORD visited Sarah as he had said, and the LORD did unto Sarah as he had spoken. For Sarah conceived, and bore Abraham a son in his old age, at the set time of which God had spoken to him. And Abraham called the name of his son that was born unto him, whom Sarah bore to him, Isaac." (Genesis 21: 1-3, NKJV)

It's amazing to me how the creator of the universe can make us promises, and yet we doubt. Nothing is impossible for God. Nothing! He promised us he would never leave us nor forsake us. He holds that promise. He was with this daughter every minute. He sealed the arteries so I wouldn't bleed to death. He provided supernatural peace, so that I would remain calm and not lose more blood. He provided the right people at the right place at the right time. He has been with me every minute of this recovery and healing. My physical and emotional self had to learn healing comes in His perfect timing, not mine.

There are plenty of scriptures that speak to us about God's timing. I hope and pray these I've included will speak to your heart as they have mine.

"But those who wait upon the LORD shall renew their strength; they shall mount up with wings as eagles; they shall run, and not be weary; and they shall walk, and not faint." (Isaiah 41:31, NKJV)

"Wait on the LORD: be of good courage, and he shall strengthen your heart: wait, I say, on the LORD." (Psalm 27:14, NKJV)

"But if we hope for that we see not, we eagerly wait for it with perseverance." (Romans 8:25, NKJV)

"Knowing that the testing of your faith produces patience." (James 1:3, NKJV)

"Strengthened with all might, according to his glorious power, for all patience and longsuffering with joy." (Colossians 1:11, NKJV)

"And to knowledge temperance; and to temperance patience; and to patience godliness." (2 Peter 1:6, KJV)

Difficult Times

I'm not going to sugarcoat it. The weeks following my accident were difficult. The nerve was taken out of my left lower leg for the radial nerve transplant. It literally took months for that leg to heal internally. There were many restless nights. These were writings that I made just before and after the radial nerve transplant surgery:

I'm sitting on my couch with external fixators through my bones, I presently can only use my right hand/arm, I've had three surgeries, I have another coming up on Wednesday, I have difficulty swallowing pills, and I am taking several a day. This does not waiver my faith and joy! I love you Jesus and give you all the glory! December 21, 2015

The pain is a different type of pain after this surgery. I guess it has something to do with the nerves. Pain medication really isn't doing much good. December 23, 2015.

The prayers worked! Sometime in the night, I went to sleep and slept for several hours, pain free. Pain is minimal this morning. God is good! December 24, 2015.

Wow! I actually got some sleep last night. Since the surgery last week, I haven't sleep well. My arm ached all night, and my hand was so swollen. Yesterday I went to the doctor and they took the surgical dressing off. It was such a relief. I realized the dressing was causing my pain. My hand swelling went down, and the pain is gone. Sleep, beautiful sleep!!!! December 31 2015.

We've had a lot of people ask if they can do anything for us. The best thing you can do is keep us lifted up in prayer. Here is our specific prayer needs:

1. No infection. External fixators are a big infection risk.
2. Radial nerve graph to start working. The doctor said it may take at least four months for the arm and brain to figure this out.
3. I have to do a special exercise every day that keeps two bones from growing together between now and the surgery in January. Prayer that these bones will do what they need to do.
4. No complications from the side effects of medication. This medication has some tough "gut" side effects. December 31, 2015.

My arm was swollen in the brace after the allograft surgery, causing a lot of pain. I couldn't get comfortable in the bed at night. I would finally get to sleep and be sleeping good and sound, and then I would move my left ankle, where the nerve was removed. The pain began, again.

When the brace was removed a few weeks after the allograft surgery, I couldn't bend my arm. Not even a millimeter. That was scary. I don't think I was prepared for that. Somewhere in the back of my mind I thought, "*When that brace comes off, my arm will work*." Being a nurse, I knew about isometric exercises. I began doing the exercises often. It didn't take long for the muscles to respond allowing me to bend my arm again. The real movement and strength came after I started physical therapy.

I Can't Swallow Those Pills

Another major struggle for me was taking medication. I literally hate taking medication. I think my brain knows that, causing me to have difficulty swallowing any pill larger than a tic tac. Of course the antibiotics to prevent infection from the external fixator were not small. I dreaded getting up every morning because I knew I would have to take those antibiotics the next day. I tried everything. I tried swallowing them with buttermilk, chocolate milk, and with a straw. I searched the Web on how to swallow a pill, and nothing worked. It was a daily fight with myself. I finally asked for the antibiotics to be filled as liquid. It was the most awful tasting medication that I've taken. I'm not sure what was worse, fighting with myself over swallowing the pills or the taste of the liquid antibiotics.

External Fixator

Being independent, it was difficult for me to allow someone to take care of me. I had difficulty dressing myself. I needed help getting in and out of the bathtub. The dressings on my wounds had to be changed, and the pin sites cleaned. I was very weak from the blood loss, so I really didn't even feel like getting out of bed many days. But, I knew I had to get out of that bed every day and move.

I carried around a very heavy external fixator on my left arm for eight weeks. It was the only thing holding my arm together. There were a few times at night, I guess moving around in my sleep, that I bloodied my nose.

Traveling back to Little Rock to the doctor with the external fixator on wasn't easy. The hardest thing was stopping at a public restroom. The fixator was heavy. It hurt my arm to let it dangle, so I held it with the other hand. Simple things like trying to lock the bathroom door, roll out toilet paper, or wash my hands became very difficult. I remember standing in the bathroom stall just crying.

The external fixator was also very large making it very difficult to put on any type of blouse. I took old T-shirts and cut the left arm out so that I would have tops to wear. It was just recently that I threw away several T-shirts without arms.

There were so many days I wanted that thing (external fixator) off my arm so bad. I felt I couldn't stand it one more minute. How did I handle those days? I tuned toward the Savior! It was all Him. He was my strength. I can do all things through Christ who strengthens me." (Philippians 4:13, NKJV) You better believe it!

Dave was so scared that he was going to rollover on my arm and hurt me while sleeping. He built a barrier in our bed between the two of us with pillows. I was sleeping under the covers, and he was sleeping on top of the covers. This lasted for at least three months. I felt sad and lonely at night not being able to be close to my husband. Dave was sensitive to that and would crawl in bed behind my back and wrap his arms around me and just hold me for a while.

Pity Party

There were several times that the old devil tried to creep in and tell me to have a pity party. There was one time in particular when I was feeling frustrated that I needed help getting a bath and getting dressed. I remember being grumpy with my husband. I was so overwhelmed I began to cry. He sat and held me and let me cry on his shoulder. I was quickly reminded by God and my loving husband that I can do this. I always bounced back quickly when reminded of my blessings. It's at those times when I felt overwhelming love from God and His supernatural peace. He never left me. I did all things through Him.

The surgery for the radial nerve transfer was on December 23rd, so we missed Christmas that year with our kids and grandkids. I just felt too bad. Again, the devil tried to creep in and throw me a party. With the love of Jesus and my husband that didn't happen. I love the post that my David made about his Christmas present that year.

Everyone has their own idea of a Christmas Present but mine is special. After the tragic event that Kathy and I went through on December 6th, I cannot think of anything in this world that I had rather have than to have my wife! Just to see her smile, hear her voice, watch her when she doesn't know I'm looking, hold her hand, kiss her lips, have a conversation with her, read the Bible with her, pray with her and the countless other things that I came close to never doing again with her! What a Christmas present God has given me, and it is all things that everyone takes for granted every day. God Bless and Merry Christmas. (December 24, 2015. David Thomas)

Dave always has a way of bringing things into perspective. This accident really brought home the true meaning of Christmas that year. We had a quite Christmas with just us two, realizing God had given us the most amazing gift.

Physical Therapy

I began physical therapy in March after the accident in December. I went to therapy two days a week from March to August. When I began therapy, I could barely bend my arm at the elbow, and I couldn't lift my arm over my shoulder. After the allograft surgery in January, I wore a brace from January to March that held my arm in place for healing. This caused my shoulder to become stiff and unusable. It took many long hours of therapy to regain the function of my elbow and shoulder.

If you're in the middle of therapy and asking if this will work. The answer is yes. Don't quit! Yes, you have to do your homework assigned by your physical therapist. It pays off. I was able to set goals and reach those goals with a lot of hard work.

The doctor told me while I was in the hospital that his goal for me was to be able to brush my hair again. I had much bigger goals. I had an anniversary coming up in May, and Dave and I had a trip planned amount Nebo. I wanted to hike the rim Trail at Mount Nebo with my husband. We also had another grandchild due to be born in August of that year. I wanted to be able to hold my new grandchild with my left arm. With God's help through lots of prayer and physical therapy, I far surpassed my physician's goal of brushing my hair and met both of my goals.

Lesson Learned

A few weeks after the accident Dave went shopping for some groceries and ran into someone we knew. She reminded him of how careless it was to have that loaded gun. She wasn't the only one that did this in the weeks to come. I struggled with putting this in my book because I want this book to be positive and uplifting. However, I learned a valuable lesson from the comments made.

We are imperfect people. We make mistakes. Sometimes we make very stupid mistakes. As Christians, Jesus teaches us to love our brother. In the middle of recovering from a crisis, an illness, or even going through something like a divorce, our brothers and sisters need our love, not our judgment. I admit it, I have done this. I have made those types of hurtful statements. This lesson is for me. I wrote this on December 29, 2015:

I normally don't let much bother me. I let most things role off my back. But not this time, I feel Ike I have to say something. I learned a valuable lesson from this. Many times when I see something on the news or hear of something happening, I might say something like, well why they didn't do this or that. Well, I won't do that again, I completely understand now. We make mistakes. We are not perfect! We have beat ourselves up over this accident many times over. Dave already hurts so bad and feels terrible. We don't need to be reminded of what we should or could have done differently. I've done this very thing with people before. Never again. Lesson learned.

He Calms the Storm

During the recovery process, we made several trips to Little Rock. We were going every two weeks in the beginning for several weeks, and then once a month for several months. Again, Satan tried to creep in, causing me to be a nervous traveler. Big cities and interstates always made me nervous. Couple that with bad weather, and I was really a nervous wreck. I know, lack of faith on my part. I was determined to conquer this lack of faith. Dave and I always said a prayer before traveling. Each time got easier, because each time God answered our prayers. We had beautiful travel days with light traffic. I began to feel total comfort and peace with the travel.

There was one day in particular that really stands out in my mind. The forecast that day was a significant chance of severe thunderstorms and even tornadoes. We left very early that morning, actually about 3:00 A.M. because I was scheduled to have a nerve transfer surgery to replace the radial nerve, and come home that same day. There were no problems at all with the weather on the way there.

While we were at the hospital, my phone rang and rang with severe thunderstorm warnings and tornado warnings. Worry and lack of faith started to creep in. God showed up as he always does. They wheeled me out to the car after my surgery and I looked up to a beautiful clear sky with the sun shining. I said, "Thank you Father, you amaze me."

Let these scriptures remind you that when the devil creeps in and tries to steal your joy and cause you to worry, you have a Father in Heaven that cares about you. You can leave all your worries with Him. Ask and He will give you peace.

"Don't worry about anything, but in everything, though prayer and petition with thanksgiving. Let your request be made known to God." (Philippians 4:6, HCSB)

"Leave all your worries with him, because He cares for you." (1 Peter 5:7, GNB)

"And with all his abundant wealth through Christ Jesus, my God will supply all your needs." (Philippians 4:19, GND)

As you can see, there were many struggles and lots of pain. God carried me through each and every one. One of the many ways he provided was by placing the right people in my path at just the right time.

Chapter Eight

Right People, Right Place, Right Time

God knows exactly what we need, right when we need it. He proved that to me over and over during my journey. Before I share with you how God provided the right people, at the right time, at the right place in my story, I'm reminded of a story that my youngest son Josh shared with me.

Josh's Story

Josh's wife, Kristine, just had a second miscarriage. They were hurting and devastated. Josh was frustrated with the world and with God. He was outside trying to put together a basketball goal, and everything was going wrong. That, coupled with his hurt, anger, and frustration, had him in a really bad place. He was having words with God. Out of nowhere a vehicle pulled in his driveway. It was the pastor of their church. He said to Josh that God laid it on his heart to come over right then and pray with him.

This was one of those pivotal moments in Josh's life, as it always is when God shows up, and your heart is open. I'm sure there are many stories just like his and mine because God provides for his children.

He Took Care of My Dave

This was an incredibly traumatic accident, and David felt responsible. There's no doubt about it, Dave was distraught. He needed consoling and he needed prayer. God provided both of those through the service of the police officer who came on the scene and the EMT who drove the ambulance to the hospital. They both prayed with David. Those prayers were incredibly comforting for David, and for me. I'm very thankful for that police officer and EMT...true public servants. Our pastor and his wife came to the emergency room and prayed with David.

All along the way, God provided people who prayed with Dave. The way God provided for David, reminds me of an Olympic runner passing the baton. With every turn of events there was someone waiting to take the baton.

Just as God provided the prayer partners for my husband Dave, He provided the right people, at the right place, at the right time for me.

Family

My son Jeremy stayed with us some that week in the hospital.

He drove from Little Rock to Oxford the night of the accident to pick up Dave's wallet and keys. He drove Dave back home on Monday to pick up our vehicle, a change of clothes, and board our dog. That was a lot of driving for his mamma, I was thankful.

The week after I came home from the hospital, my daughter Amy came and spent the day with me. She left her babies at home so she could dedicate the whole day to taking care of her mamma. I cherish that day. She cooked food for me. We sat and talked. I think not being able to be with me in the hospital after the accident, she needed that day as much as I did. It was a blessing that I'll never forget.

With the accident happening in December, it was cold outside. I couldn't wear a coat because of the external fixator. Dave and I had to travel back and forth to Little Rock a lot. I needed a way to stay warm. My son Josh and daughter-in-law Kristine found me a beautiful heavy sweater that had huge armholes that would fit over the fixator. I loved it. It was one of those warm and cozy sweaters. Sometimes it's the small things that are big to the one receiving them.

I also remember Josh, Kristine and Isaac standing outside, watching me, as I was being loaded onto to the helicopter. They handed Dave a jacket for the helicopter ride. The love and support was much needed and appreciated.

David's niece Ashley worked for a local pharmacy and she always made sure that I had my medication, always bringing the medications right to our home.

Caregivers

Every step of the way, God provided. He provided just the right paramedic, nurses, physicians, surgeons, and physical therapist. I needed a paramedic that was highly skilled; one that knew the pathophysiology of shock, blood loss, and pain. She knew that I was in extreme pain and wanted to provide me comfort and pain control. She also knew that with my blood pressure being so low from the blood loss, pain medication could compromise my life. She knew to reapply the tourniquet with the dropping of my blood pressure and to increase the fluids, all the while keeping me totally informed of everything she was doing. I felt very blessed to be in her care.

Holly was the house supervisor at the hospital that day. When I asked Dave to hand me my cell phone so I could call the hospital and let them know what was happening, I was very comforted to hear Holly's voice on the other end of line. We had worked together for a number of years, and I knew she would work very hard to get the people I needed in the building for my arrival.

Dr. Allen is highly skilled and has worked at WRMC for a number of years. I knew that if Dr. Allen had faith and confidence in the surgeon he was sending me to, so should I. Dr. Abraham had a very comforting voice; he said we're going to take good care of you. Just the right words I needed to hear at that moment.

With the complexity of this wound and all the damage to the bones, joints, inner workings of the elbow, God knew it would take a highly skilled, specialized surgeon…one that could take an arm in many pieces and put it back together. He provided.

Dr. Ahmadi from UAMS, Medical Center did an amazing job putting my elbow back together. The result is a fully functional elbow; an elbow that allows me to play basketball with the grandkids.

God provided great nurses through Survival Flight, WRMC, and UAMS, Medical Center. They were highly skilled in knowledge and providing compassionate, patient centered care.

Katrina was the flight pilot. She was confident in her role and it shined through in her words. She managed herself up as she introduced herself to me and told me how many years she had flown in the military. She said she would take be taking good care of me as we flew to Little Rock. I took great comfort in her words. She was spot on. We had a smooth twenty-five minute flight to Little Rock.

I needed a physical therapist who would speak to my heart and motivate me. I needed a physical therapist with a heart for Jesus. It was going to be a long road to recovery. He provided.

Benjamin Lambert was my physical therapist. I knew from the very first day that I started therapy, there was something very special about Benjamin. He was kind, compassionate, and worked very hard to teach me just what I needed to know to make sure this arm would work right again. He had to do his homework. I'm quite sure he had never taken care of someone with this type of injury. I could tell he had the heart of a servant, and that he loved Jesus.

Benjamin and I talked openly about our faith and our families. When I think about Benjamin this scripture comes to mind: "Let your light so shine before men, that they may see your good works, and glorify your Father which is in Heaven." (Matthew 5:16, NKJV) I knew that God had a hand in this relationship. Benjamin was my physical therapist, but he became my friend. He is my brother in Christ.

Several months after the accident, I was working on a presentation about my story for a women's conference at our church. I remembered someone in the emergency room taking a picture of the x-ray of my arm and showing it to me, but I couldn't remember who took the picture.

I wanted a copy of that picture for my presentation. I asked several people in the emergency room if they remembered who took the picture and no one could remember. I gave up on asking others about the picture and decided to pray about it instead, asking

God to help me find that picture.

After returning to work, I was doing some safety rounding on one of the nursing units. I saw Dr. Abraham standing at the nurses' station. I said, "Do you remember me?" He stood there a minute, and I said, "The gunshot in the arm." He reached over, grabbed me, and gave me a big bear hug. We talked for just a minute as he asked me how I was doing. Out of the blue, he said, "I still have the picture of the x-ray on my phone." A big smile came to my face. I cried on the way home from work that day as I told God thank you for answering that prayer for me. Things that are important to us are important to God, no matter how small.

Brothers and Sisters

Brother John Hodges is our pastor. I think he and his wife sister Sandy were waiting on us when the ambulance arrived in the emergency room. If not it was shortly thereafter. He also came to Little Rock that night. He and my son Jeremy were there to support and comfort Dave while I was in surgery. He came back to Little Rock, while I was in the hospital to see us, minister to us, and pray for us. He stopped by our home often to make sure our needs were being met.

Our church family fed us emotionally, spiritually, and physically. Brother John told Dave they gathered together at the outdoor drama at our church the night of the accident and prayed for me. He answered! "For where two or three are gathered in my name, I am there in the midst of them." (Matthew 18:20) While I was in the hospital and for months after, we received many phone calls, cards, and prayers from our brothers and sisters in Christ.

We were getting ready to go home after being in the hospital for a week. I was extremely fatigued from the blood loss and surgeries. Dave was worn out from lack of sleep and stress. The dietitian had been in my room before discharge and told me that I need to be eating well to help this wound heal. I started to cry and asked Dave, "What are we going to do?" We didn't have any food in the house. I knew I didn't have the energy to cook, and he was worn-out. We had just started moving into the house when the accident happened. Not only did we not have food, we didn't have anything except our bed and living room furniture moved over yet. We had nothing there to even prepare a meal.

When we got home on Friday, our church family started bringing food and brought it every day. We had homemade vegetable soup, cornbread, meatballs, meatloaf, chili, fried chicken, salad, macaroni and cheese, all types of vegetables and desserts.

Our church family filled our tummies and our spirit. I can't tell you how much that touched our hearts and comforted us in so many ways. What a blessing! We had many visits from our brothers and sisters. Each visit brought lots of love and prayers that were very comforting.

There were so many people who touched our lives during this time. I think about Rob and Carrie and the turkey and cheese that they brought for us to eat. I was often nauseous and that cold turkey rolled up with cheese was the only thing I could eat first thing in the morning. Jimalee's macaroni and cheese was amazing and such comfort food as was Avis's spaghetti. Rita's soup and salad along with her smile and kind voice warmed our heart. This was just a few of the long list of our brothers and sisters who kept us fed.

Friends

Our dear friends Kathy and Kevin Luke came to see me not long after I came home from the hospital. Kathy and I have been friends since the second grade. It always fills my heart with joy to see her. She made me a beautiful cross wreath. It was meant to hang on the front door, but I was afraid it would get weathered or blown off, so I hung it in our war room. I think of Kathy every time I go in there to pray.

When Dave boarded our dog, the guy at the kennel told Dave he and his wife were praying for me. The teller at our bank told Dave the same. Dave called Paula from the Human Resources Department at my work about health insurance maters. She was kind and professional to Dave and made sure everything was in order, telling him to not worry about anything. That was very comforting to both of us.

My friend and co-worker Tina, brought me some goodies that she made, they were packed with protein and nutrients to help my wound healing. Mr. Paxson, my administrator, was so supportive and always said he was praying for me.

Our friends Larry and Judy called us often, prayed for us, and sent us money in the mail because they knew the expense of travel and Dave buying meals at the hospital.

Our neighbor, Mrs. Ward made soup and stopped by several times to see if she could help us in any way.

After being home and unable to work for several weeks, I began to feel a little down. It had been months since I had been able to get to my gray colored. Dave suggested that he could drive me to get my hair done and make me feel better. I took him up on that offer.

My hairstylist and friend Natalie did my hair that day as she listened to my story. I saw concern and compassion in her eyes. When she was finished, I felt so much better. When I got ready to pay she said no I've got this one. There were tears in both of our eyes. I needed that lift in my spirit that day. I think it was a combination of being able to tell my story and doing something for me that made me feel better. I am thankful for my friend Natalie.

I could go on and on, so many people were uplifting and praying for us. I fear I have left someone out in my story. Please forgive me if I have. I'm very thankful for each and every person who God put in the right place at the right time.

It amazes me how everything fell into place in this journey. It's absolutely too perfect. There is no way this is chance. Luck? No way. Being a child of God and His power is what got me through this journey. His Perfect Work was at hand.

Chapter Nine

His Perfect Work

Very soon after the accident I felt God speaking to my heart. He wanted me to tell my story. His story. On December 10th, four days after my accident, I wrote this:

I feel in my heart that God wants me to use this tragedy to speak to others and to witness. I am so full of hope! I love this scripture. "Through Him we have also obtained access by faith into this grace in which we stand, and we rejoice in hope of all the glory of God. Not only that, but we rejoice in our sufferings, knowing that suffering produces endurance, and endurance produces character, and character produces hope, and hope does not put us to shame, because God's love has been poured into our hearts through the Holy Spirit who has been given to us." (Romans 5:2 – 5 ESV)

I felt like God was leading me to tell my story. I asked the leader in charge of our yearly Women's Conference at our church if I could speak at our conference to give my testimony about the accident. It was several months away. She told me no, the agenda was already set. I prayed about it, and asked God if He wasn't really speaking to my heart, if I wanted to tell this story for my own selfish reasons, for Him to reveal it to me.

I still felt led, so I prayed for God to provide me the platform. I didn't really give it much thought in the weeks to come; instead I focused on my healing and recovery. A few months later, the women's group at church told me I was on the agenda to present my testimony about my accident at our annual Women's Conference. He answered my prayer with His timing, not mine. God is good.

Several months after the accident I was driving home from work thinking about what to call my presentation at the Women's Conference. How do I sum up what happened and give it a title? Out of nowhere, while sitting silently in my car, the title came to me. *His Perfect Work!* Have you ever noticed that sometimes when we're quiet and still God speaks to us? The problem is, in this day and age, we're often not quiet or still.

Goosebumps Moment

The morning of the Women's Conference I was looking at my presentation one more time to ensure it was polished up. A song kept coming in my head. The song was, "Eye of The Storm". I told Dave, "I feel like God wants me to add this song to my presentation." He said, "If that's how you feel, you better do it." I added the song to my presentation.

It was only a few minutes after the main speaker began that morning at the Women's Conference that I realized God had his hand in this conference. It was a goose bumps moment. The speaker was talking about how to get through the storms of life. Each one of the speakers at the conference had the same theme. It was as if we had met prior to the conference to have a united front. I knew in that moment why He wanted the song. It was perfect.

His perfect work. That's it. That sums it up. From the moment that gun discharged, He was at work. It was and is His perfect work. Everything was too perfect. Nothing was luck.

I'm Not Lucky

You are so lucky! The phrase I heard over and over through this journey. If luck is defined as happening by chance, then I don't believe luck had anything to do with the events that occurred during my journey. The Bible tells us that God provides.

"Every good gift and every perfect gift is from above, coming down from the Father of lights with whom there is no variation or shadow of turning." (James 1:17, NKJV)

"He will never leave us nor forsake us." (Hebrews 13:5, KNJV)

He provided and He never left me. He carried me through and is still carrying me through.

He Provided

God saved my life that day, and my arm. He provided me the strength to endure the pain. He provided me the supernatural peace that passes all understanding. He provided the belt. He controlled the trajectory of the bullet. He protected the arteries. He put the right people in the right place at the right time. He provided the police officer and the EMT who prayed with my husband Dave. He guided the surgeon's hands. He brought me a new friend, brother in Christ, and physical therapists.

He protected the helicopter flight, the ambulance ride, and the many, many trips to Little Rock and back. He held back the weather and calmed the stormy skies. He showed up at the Women's Conference when I was providing my testimony. He held me up sitting at that picnic table in Sam's Club. He provided comfort through our family, our pastors, our brothers and sisters in Christ, and the hospital chaplain at UAMS, Medical Center.

He provided perfect healing of my wounds. He prevented complications during and after five surgeries. He comforted me as I cried in my bed, feeling overwhelmed knowing how much God loves me.

He provided me the platforms to tell my story. His story. He put my face on billboards, on jumbotrons, on television, in magazines, and in newspapers. He showed me how to get my testimony in print and out to the world.

Divine Providence

My dear friend Sue recently told me that my story is a perfect example of divine providence. I believe with all my heart she is absolutely right. Divine providence, is defined as God's intervention in the world.

Recently Dave was cleaning out his old truck and found the bag of items that was sent home from the hospital with me that first week. It had my clothing that I was wearing at the time of the accident, a blanket, and the large pad that was under my back while on the stretcher in the emergency room. I'm really not sure why they sent that home with us. Maybe it was meant for us to see it a year and a half later. The clothing was completely covered and stained with blood as was the pad that had been underneath me. Seeing the amount of blood was a reminder of God's divine providence.

I can't finish this book without asking my readers this question. Are you letting God do perfect work in your life? He can. He will, if you will allow. Are you holding a grudge? Has someone hurt you and you have stored up anger? Let Him do a perfect work in your life to heal that anger and pain.

The story of Joseph comes to mind. If anyone had the right to hold a grudge, it was Joseph. He was thrown into a well and sold into slavery by his brothers when he was a young man. Many years later he was the ruler of the nation, and he could've killed his brothers or had his brothers killed, but he spared them. He forgave them. Joseph is a great example of God's perfect work; of divine providence. Joseph's heart was open and he let God do perfect work and his life. The Bible is full of stories where God has done His perfect work. He put those examples in Bible for us.

Be Still

One of the things I have learned in my recovery time, from this accident is, be still. What does that mean? What does that look like? It means slowdown, sit quietly, and listen to the Holy Spirit. This accident caused me to take a hard look at my life…the busyness of my life. I heard a preacher on the radio say that busyness is a "soul sucker". I believe that to be true. I've made the statement too many times, "that sucks the life out of me." God helps us with soul restoration. He makes us lie down in green pastures.

The LORD *is* my shepherd;
I shall not want.
He makes me to lie down in green pastures;
He leads me beside the still waters.

He restores my soul;

He leads me in the paths of righteousness

For His name's sake.

Yea, though I walk through the valley of the shadow of death,

I will fear no evil;

For You *are* with me;

Your rod and Your staff, they comfort me.

You prepare a table before me in the presence of my enemies;

You anoint my head with oil;

My cup runs over.

Surely goodness and mercy shall follow me

All the days of my life;

And I will dwell in the house of the LORD

Forever. (Psalm 23, NKJV)

In May of last year, Dave and I took a trip to Mount Nebo Arkansas. The mountain is named after Mount Nebo in the Bible because of the incredible view. Dave and I spent a week there just practicing being still. It was an incredible way to reconnect with God and the beauty of this planet He created.

I am more focused now. God first. Family second. Job third. God did His perfect work not only on my physical body but on my mental health. I needed a little redirection.

Keep Your Eyes on Jesus

We have a basketball goal in our backyard. When the weather permits, I go out and shoot hoops every day. I shoot until I make 20 baskets. In the beginning that took a while; now, not so much. I feel drawn to that basketball goal. It is such a sense of accomplishment, making those baskets. Each basket reminds me of the healing and miracles that God provided. I shoot those baskets because I can.

One day Dave was watching me, and I was missing every basket. He said, "You're taking your eyes off of square behind the basket. Keep your eyes on that square." I did. I made the next basket, and the next. There were many times during this journey that I wanted to take my eyes off of the square…the square being Jesus. Each time I took my eyes off Him, for even a minute, fear would creep in. I cried lots of tears and said lots of prayers. He always answered. He always provided peace.

Have you been through trauma? Has someone hurt you as a child or an adult? Are you hurting from grief, divorce, or maybe you're addicted to drugs or alcohol? Maybe you think you're just too bad. Are you broken? God can put the pieces back together if you will open your heart. These are the moments in life where we make the decision to turn away from God or run to Him.

I heard a quote by Charles Spurgeon, "Sometimes God has to break you into pieces to make you." He will do His perfect work in your life. Remember His grace is sufficient for you. God is enough. He will help you through things that are unbearable without him.

"Call to me when trouble comes; I will save you, and you will praise me." (Psalm 50:15, GNB)

"But his answer was: "My grace is all you need, for my power is greatest when you are weak." I am most happy, then, to be proud of my weaknesses, in order to feel the protection of Christ's power over me." (2 Corinthians 12:9, GNB)

I love this story about Paul and Silas. It reminds us that our joy does not come from our present circumstances. Beaten, battered, I'm sure horrible surroundings, they were praying and singing. How many times do we let our circumstances rob us of our joy? Not only were they singing and praying, their present circumstance allowed them to witness to the jailer, causing him and his family to be saved.

"And when they had laid many stripes on them, they threw them into prison, commanding the jailer to keep them securely. Having received such a charge, he put them into the inner prison and fastened their feet in the stocks. But at midnight Paul and Silas were praying and singing hymns to God, and the prisoners were listening to them." (Acts 16:23-25, NKJV)

Rise on Wings Like Eagles

I was listening to the radio on the way home from work this week when I heard a preacher talk about eagles. He quoted scriptures out of Isaiah. "He strengthens those who are weak and tired." (Isaiah 40:29, GNB)

"But those who trust in the LORD for help will find their strength renewed. They will rise on wings like eagles; they will run and not get weary; they will walk and not grow weak." (Isaiah 40:31, GNB)

The preacher said that eagles love a good storm. He said eagles will fly high above the storm and let the wind lift them and give them more speed above the storm. Normally they can fly around 50 miles an hour, but above a storm they can fly speeds in excess of 100 miles an hour.

While I did not enjoy the middle of the storm, it did lift me higher and closer to God. Wait upon the Lord and he will give you strength to rise above the storm. He will do His perfect work in your life.

Chapter Ten

I'm Not Lucky, I'm Blessed

Snapshots

When I read a book, I love to look at pictures that make the story more personal and real. This chapter is a collection of pictures that I hope will sum up my story and show that I never lost my joy.

One last thing...

"Rejoice in hope; be patient in affliction; be persistent in prayer." (Romans 12:12, HCSB)

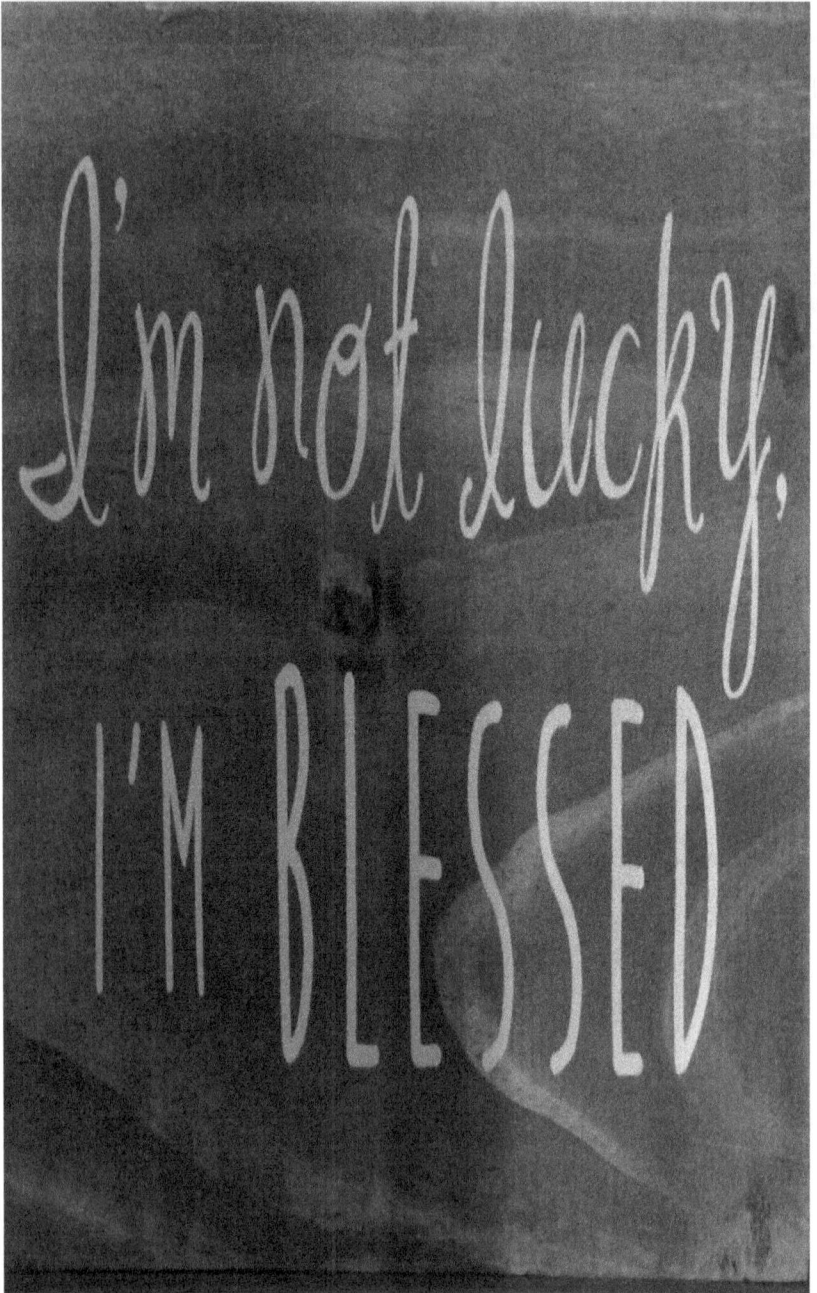

How I feel every day!

The sign Dave placed in our driveway after the accident. Yes it is.

The cap I was wearing at the time of the accident. Backwards…

The belt, where it was hanging, when Dave found it. Miracle.

Doctor's goal. Met.

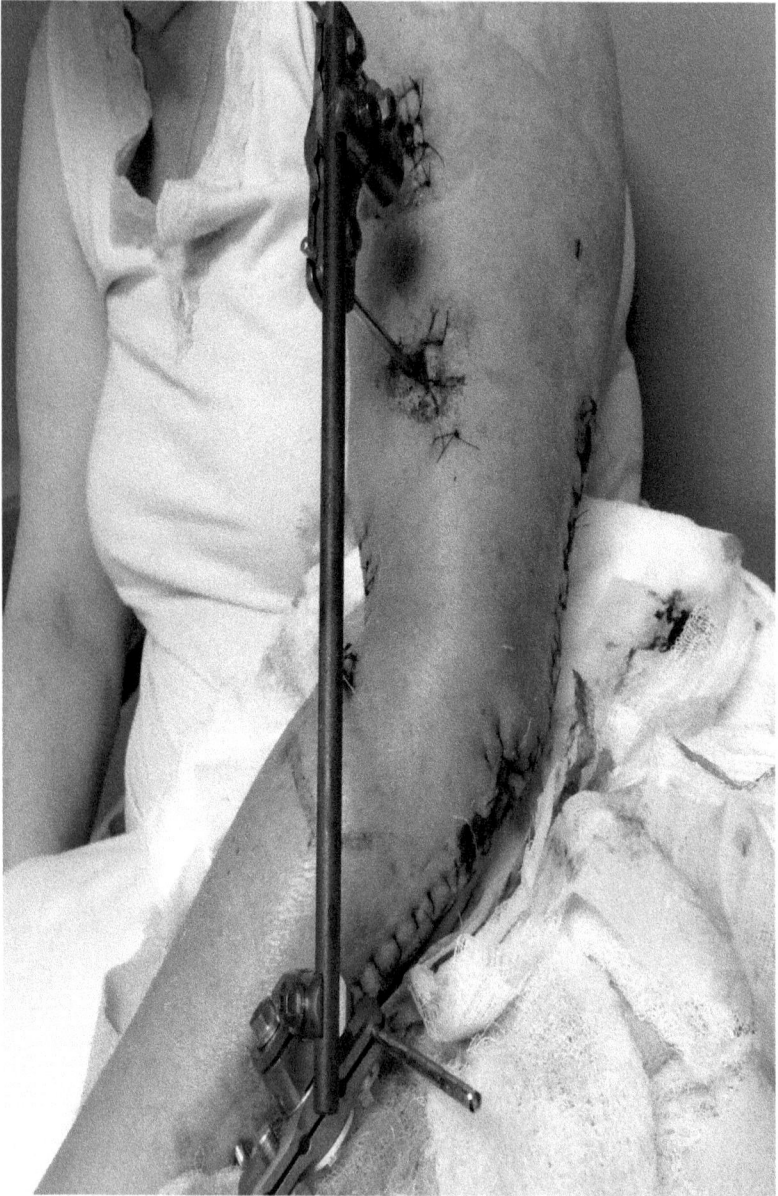

External fixator holding everything together, to allow healing.

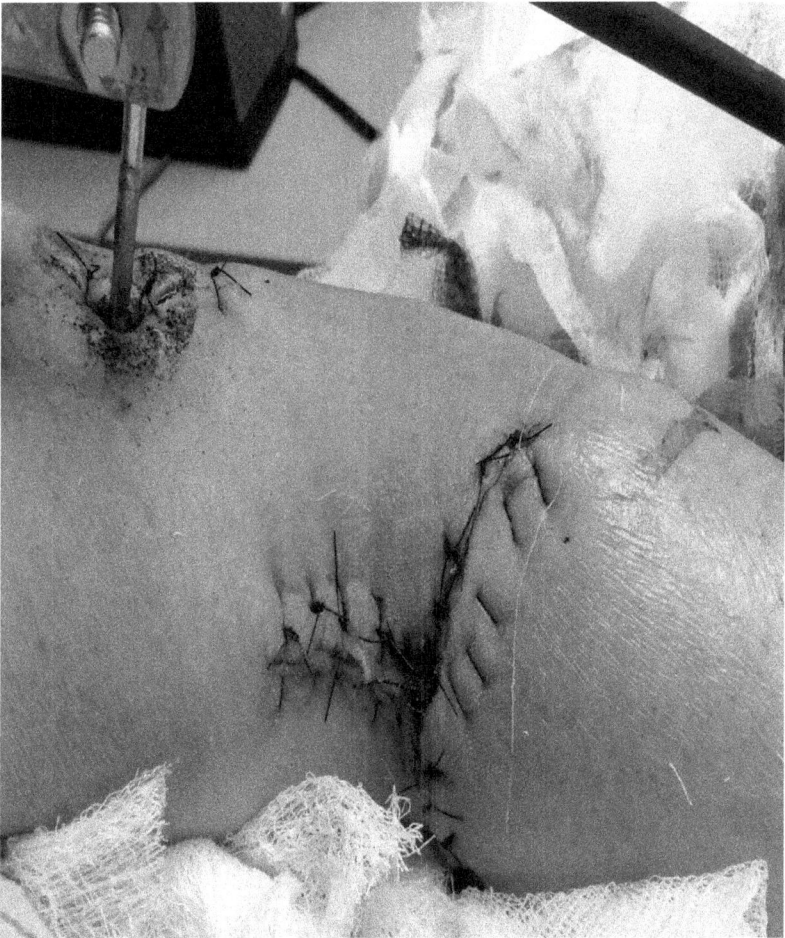

Close up of the inner elbow.

The cards and letters that I received. Fuel for the soul.

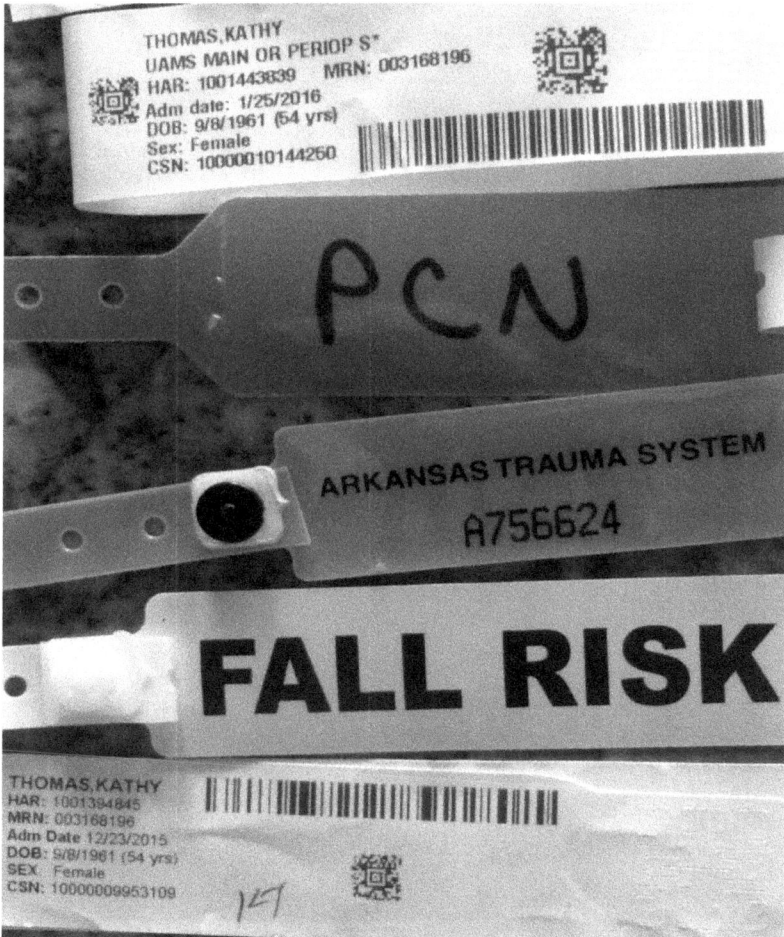

Various memorabilia worn during hospital stays.

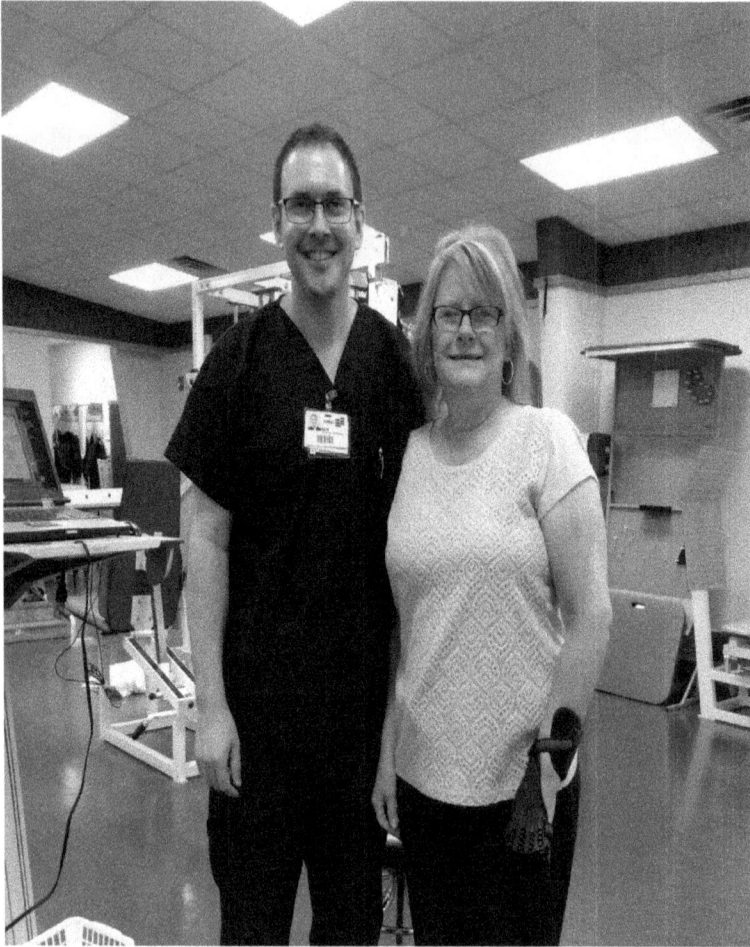

My Brother in Christ and Physical therapist, Benjamin.

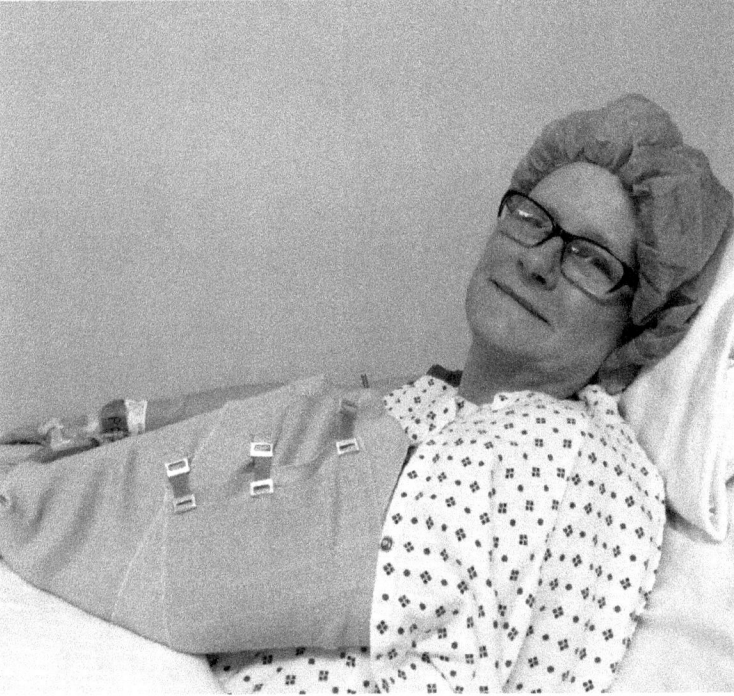

Just before I went into the nerve transfer surgery. At Peace.

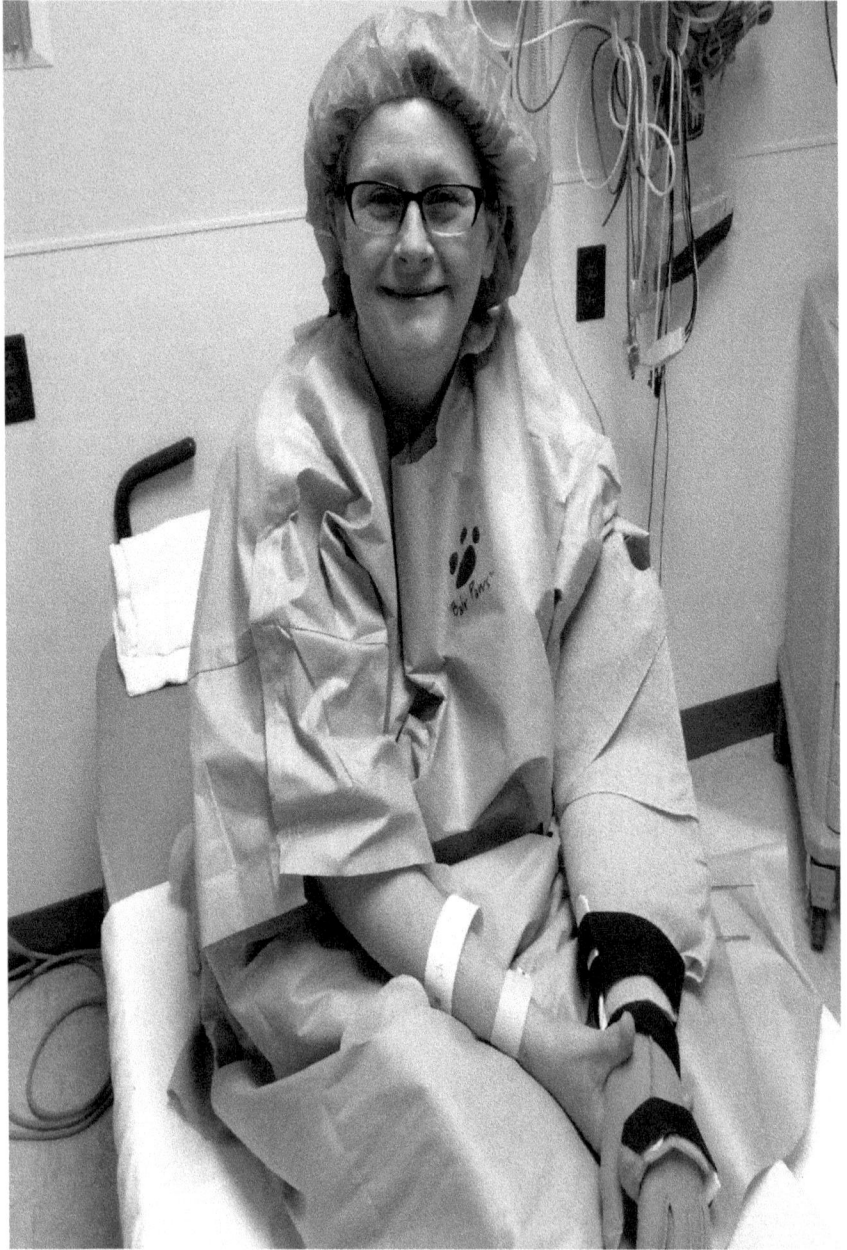

Just before the allograft surgery. Smile of joy.

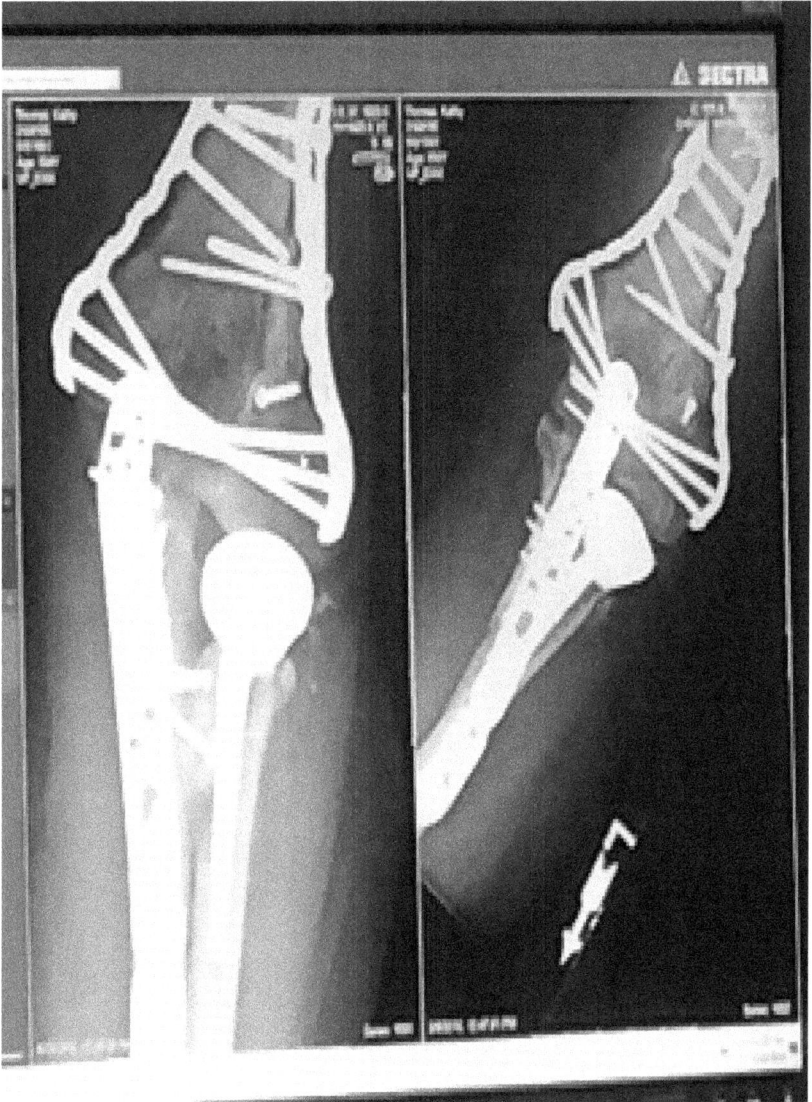

X-ray after the allograft surgery. Lots of hardware. I wonder what's going to happen when I go through the airport scanner.

David and Kathy one year later, December 2016. Happy.

This picture was taken in May 2016 at Mount Nebo, Arkansas, after the accident in December, 2015. Dave and I were celebrating our anniversary and taking some time…to be still.

Physical therapy from March 2016 to August 2016. Perseverance.

My goal met. Me, holding our new Granddaughter, Sadie Mae. Using my left arm. August 2016. Love.

ABOUT THE AUTHOR

KATHY IS A MASTERS PREPARED REGISTERED NURSE. SHE AND HER HUSBAND, DAVE, HAVE SIX KIDS, AND 18 GRANDKIDS. THEY RESIDE IN OXFORD, ARKANSAS. ABOVE ALL ELSE, SHE LOVES THE LORD. SHE PLANS TO DONATE ALL PROFIT FROM THIS BOOK TO VARIOUS CHARITIES.